SAVING ANIMALS
SAVING
POLAR BEARS

by Emma Huddleston

T0014925

FOCUS
READERS.

NAVIGATOR

WWW.FOCUSREADERS.COM

Focus Readers is distributed by North Star Editions:
sales@northstareditions.com | 888-417-0195

Produced for Focus Readers by Red Line Editorial.

Content Consultant: Andrew E. Derocher, PhD, Professor of Biological Sciences, University of Alberta

Photographs ©: Shutterstock Images, cover, 1, 7, 10–11, 13 (shrimp-like animals, Arctic foxes, rodents, plants, algae, fish, ringed seal, seabirds), 15, 16–17, 22–23; iStockphoto, 4–5, 9, 13 (polar bear and background), 25; Linette Boisvert/NASA, 19; Paul Nicklen/SeaLegacy/Zuma Press/Newscom, 21; Konrad Wothe/Minden Pictures/Newscom, 27; Bonnie Jo Mount/The Washington Post/Getty Images, 29

Library of Congress Cataloging-in-Publication Data
Names: Huddleston, Emma, author.
Title: Saving polar bears / Emma Huddleston.
Description: Lake Elmo, MN : Focus Readers, [2021] | Series: Saving animals | Includes index. | Audience: Grades 4-6
Identifiers: LCCN 2019057387 (print) | LCCN 2019057388 (ebook) | ISBN 9781644933893 (hardcover) | ISBN 9781644934654 (paperback) | ISBN 9781644936177 (pdf) | ISBN 9781644935415 (ebook)
Subjects: LCSH: Polar bear--Conservation--Juvenile literature.
Classification: LCC QL737.C27 H83 2021 (print) | LCC QL737.C27 (ebook) | DDC 599.786--dc23
LC record available at https://lccn.loc.gov/2019057387
LC ebook record available at https://lccn.loc.gov/2019057388

Printed in the United States of America
Mankato, MN
012021

ABOUT THE AUTHOR

Emma Huddleston lives in the Twin Cities with her husband. She enjoys writing children's books, running, and reading novels. She loves learning about animals and ways people are working to help them!

TABLE OF CONTENTS

CHAPTER 1

ARCTIC GIANTS

Polar bears live in the Arctic. The Arctic is one of the coldest places on Earth. But polar bears have **adapted** to the harsh climate. For instance, polar bears rely on their thick coats. They also have a layer of fat known as blubber. These layers of fur and blubber help polar bears keep warm.

In parts of the Arctic, the average temperature in January can be –29 degrees Fahrenheit (–34°C).

In addition, pregnant polar bears dig snow dens in the winter. They give birth in the dens and raise their cubs there. Dens are safe from harsh weather.

Polar bears are marine animals. They are sometimes called sea bears because they depend on the ocean more than the land to survive. Polar bears walk on ice

MELTING ICE

When the ice melts during the warm summer months, many polar bears live on land. Some move south. Others move north. They travel to northern parts of North America, Europe, and Asia. Some of these areas are tundra. The tundra is like a cold desert at all times of the year.

and swim between ice chunks. They travel thousands of miles each year to find food. They look for places with water channels or cracks in the ice. These locations are the best for hunting seals. Life for other Arctic animals would change without polar bears at the top of the **food web**.

POLAR BEAR RANGE, 2019

RUSSIA

NORWAY

ALASKA

GREENLAND

CANADA

STAYING WARM

Polar bears must keep their bodies the right temperature. Their coats protect them from cold Arctic air. Each bear's coat is made of two layers. Long hairs make up the top layer. Underneath, there is a layer of short, fuzzy hair. Together, these layers can be up to 2 inches (5 cm) thick. A polar bear's coat has no color. It looks white because of the way it reflects light.

Under its skin, a polar bear has a layer of blubber. This blubber can be more than 4 inches (10 cm) thick. Blubber **insulates** the bear's body. Despite living in the Arctic, polar bears can easily overheat. As a result, they move slowly and rest often. Sometimes they need to cool off. They swim or lie down in the snow.

Polar bears can survive in temperatures as cold as −50 degrees Fahrenheit (−46°C).

CHAPTER 2

TOP OF THE FOOD WEB

Polar bears have no natural predators. They are at the top of the food web in the Arctic marine ecosystem. An ecosystem is all of the living things that share a habitat. Top predators play an important role in ecosystems. They eat other species. They help keep the **populations** of other species in balance.

Polar bears mainly eat ringed seals.

Without top predators, other animals in the food web could change the ecosystem. For example, too many **herbivores** could eat too much of a plant species. In an ecosystem, each species depends on others to survive.

SIGNS OF HEALTH

Algae is the base of the Arctic food web. It grows on the underside of sea ice. Small shrimp-like animals eat the algae. Fish eat these animals. Seals eat the fish. Polar bears eat the seals. But as sea ice melts, the amount of algae changes. Each level of the food web is affected. Since polar bears are at the top of the food web, they are a sign of how the ecosystem is doing. If polar bears are struggling, it is a sign that the ecosystem is changing.

Polar bears are powerful predators. Their main food source is seals. They can smell seals from far away. Polar bears have strong senses of smell. Sometimes they can smell seals that are under snow.

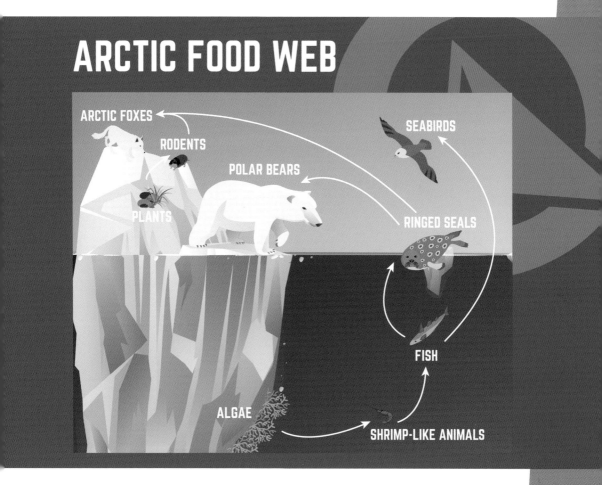

ARCTIC FOOD WEB

ARCTIC FOXES
RODENTS
PLANTS
POLAR BEARS
SEABIRDS
RINGED SEALS
FISH
ALGAE
SHRIMP-LIKE ANIMALS

Seals are the only food with enough fat to keep polar bears healthy. But sometimes polar bears cannot find seals. This tends to happen during warm seasons with less ice. However, bears can survive long periods without food. They can use their thick fat layers for energy.

During these times, polar bears may also eat other animals. They may kill walruses. They may find dead whales that wash onto shore. Sometimes bears eat bird eggs out of nests on the ground. In Norway, scientists found that polar bears ate up to 90 percent of the eggs in a nesting **colony**. Bird populations suffer from polar bears raiding their nests.

The fur of an Arctic fox helps it stay warm and blend in with its surroundings.

Without polar bears, other animals may struggle to survive. For example, Arctic foxes sometimes rely on polar bears. Thick snow covers the ground during winter. As a result, hunting rodents is difficult for foxes. So, the foxes follow polar bears and eat their leftovers. Some foxes need polar bears to make it through the winter.

CHAPTER 3

FACING THREATS

Scientists try to count polar bear populations. However, polar bears live far north in remote areas. Sometimes females disappear into dens for several months. One tracking method uses helicopters or small planes. Scientists fly over areas where polar bears could be. But they do not always see bears.

Polar bear dens can be as warm as 40 degrees Fahrenheit (4.4°C), even in the middle of winter.

Scientists have also tried counting polar bears from space using **satellites**.

For all these reasons, tracking polar bears is expensive. As a result, scientists do not have accurate numbers for past polar bear populations. However, scientists are still concerned. They know

FAT AND ENERGY

Polar bears need to store enough fat to survive times when they cannot hunt. If ice disappears before polar bears get enough food, they can die. Females need to store extra fat to raise newborn cubs. Mothers must weigh at least 440 pounds (200 kg). Small cubs or cubs with skinny mothers are more likely to die during their first year.

Between 1979 and 2018, the Arctic lost more than 10 trillion tons (9.1 trillion metric tons) of floating ice.

some populations have declined. They also know sea ice is melting.

Climate change is raising average temperatures on Earth. This change is causing sea ice to melt earlier in the year.

The ice is freezing later, too. As a result, polar bears spend less time on sea ice every year.

Polar bears depend on sea ice in many ways. For instance, polar bears hunt seals on sea ice. They can rest and save energy while they wait for seals. Without sea ice, bears use extra energy for hunting. They travel farther for food or mating. They may catch fewer seals. With less food, polar bears risk starving.

The loss of sea ice also threatens polar bears in other ways. It disrupts the whole Arctic ecosystem. For example, with less ice, less algae grows. Or algae changes so it can grow in areas without ice. Then, the

A polar bear can lose 15 pounds (6.8 kg) of fat each week it does not hunt.

animals that eat the algae must move and change, too. These changes affect other animals in the food web. Eventually, polar bears can be affected as well.

CHAPTER 4

PROTECTING POLAR BEARS

To help polar bears, scientists are studying the animals and their habitats. Some scientists track female polar bears by using collars. The collars use satellites to track the bears' locations. Then they send that data to scientists' computers. This kind of tracking lets scientists see where bears go and when.

A polar bear wears a tracking collar on the Svalbard Islands of Norway.

Studying polar bear movement can help people make decisions. Scientists find out how human activity helps or harms polar bears.

In addition, some governments use laws to protect polar bears. Canada, Greenland, and the United States all limit polar bear hunting. Norway and most of Russia ban hunting completely. In Norway, hunting polar bears has been banned since 1973. This area lost a large amount of its sea ice between the 1980s and 2010s. But the number of polar bears there remained steady. Some scientists believe the ban on hunting is one reason why.

In 2017, the US government started trying to open up the Arctic National Wildlife Refuge in Alaska to oil drilling.

Governments protect polar bears in other ways, too. In Alaska, communities and wildlife experts monitor the coast. They try to keep polar bears safe when the bears go near cities.

Countries across the Arctic have created protected areas for polar bears. Human activity is limited in these places. Protected areas help keep polar bears safe and living in their natural habitat.

People in Manitoba, Canada, have taken action to protect polar bears. Wildlife officers stand watch for polar bears in towns. They don't kill a polar bear that comes too close. Instead, they try to chase the bear away. They may set off firecrackers or shoot guns without bullets. The loud noises often scare the polar bear away. But sometimes the bear stays put. When that happens, officers put it in a polar bear jail. A polar bear jail is a safe building for bears to stay in. Later, officers guide the bear back into the wild.

Laws and community actions help polar bears. However, they cannot stop

For both the people's and the polar bears' protection, a helicopter carries two bears to polar bear jail.

sea ice from melting. Polar bears rely on the sea ice to survive. To save polar bears, people must slow climate change.

Everyone can help by using less energy. They also can demand that their governments take action. National governments must make massive changes, such as changing their energy sources.

People must protect polar bears and their habitats. For that reason, scientists continue to study polar bear habitats. Many study sea ice and how it is changing. These scientists often study groups of bears that live farther south than other groups. Areas farther south are warmer. As a result, sea ice melt is greater in those areas. But sea ice is changing all over the Arctic. Learning

Scientists use a tool to take Arctic ice samples in 2019.

about southern bear populations may help scientists understand how sea ice melt will impact other polar bear groups.

Polar bears are facing many threats. Even so, a large number of people are staying focused on saving them.

FOCUS ON
SAVING
POLAR BEARS

Write your answers on a separate piece of paper.

1. Write a letter to a friend describing some of the threats that polar bears face.

2. Do you think hunting polar bears should be banned in all places? Why or why not?

3. What animals make up most of a polar bear's diet?
   - **A.** seals
   - **B.** birds
   - **C.** whales

4. How might tracking polar bears help scientists protect them?
   - **A.** Scientists can find paths for polar bears to leave the Arctic.
   - **B.** Scientists can stop polar bears before they reach dangerous places.
   - **C.** Scientists can learn which areas matter most to polar bears and protect those areas.

Answer key on page 32.

GLOSSARY

adapted
Changed over time to deal with a certain situation.

algae
Tiny, plant-like organisms that produce oxygen.

climate change
A human-caused global crisis involving long-term changes in Earth's temperature and weather patterns.

colony
A group of animals that live together.

food web
The feeding relationships among different living things.

herbivores
Animals that eat mostly plants.

insulates
Stops heat from getting in or out.

populations
Groups of animals living in particular areas.

satellites
Objects or vehicles that orbit a planet or moon, often to collect information.

TO LEARN MORE

BOOKS

Borgert-Spaniol, Megan. *Polar Bears.* Minneapolis: Abdo Publishing, 2019.

Gagne, Tammy. *Polar Bears Matter.* Minneapolis: Abdo Publishing, 2016.

Marquardt, Meg. *Polar Bears on the Hunt.* Minneapolis: Lerner Publications, 2018.

NOTE TO EDUCATORS

Visit **www.focusreaders.com** to find lesson plans, activities, links, and other resources related to this title.

INDEX

Answer Key: 1. Answers will vary; **2.** Answers will vary; **3.** A; **4.** C